AF228565

Rocky Mountain
National Park

by Grace Hansen

Abdo Kids Jumbo is an Imprint of Abdo Kids
abdobooks.com

abdobooks.com

Published by Abdo Kids, a division of ABDO, P.O. Box 398166, Minneapolis, Minnesota 55439.
Copyright © 2019 by Abdo Consulting Group, Inc. International copyrights reserved in all countries.
No part of this book may be reproduced in any form without written permission from the publisher.
Abdo Kids Jumbo™ is a trademark and logo of Abdo Kids.

102018

012019

THIS BOOK CONTAINS
RECYCLED MATERIALS

Photo Credits: Alamy, iStock, Shutterstock

Production Contributors: Teddy Borth, Jennie Forsberg, Grace Hansen

Design Contributors: Dorothy Toth, Laura Mitchell

Library of Congress Control Number: 2018946059
Publisher's Cataloging-in-Publication Data

Names: Hansen, Grace, author.

Title: Rocky Mountain National Park / by Grace Hansen.

Description: Minneapolis, Minnesota : Abdo Kids, 2019 | Series: National parks
    Includes glossary, index and online resources (page 24).

Identifiers: ISBN 9781532182099 (lib. bdg.) | ISBN 9781532183072 (ebook) |
    ISBN 9781532183560 (Read-to-me ebook)

Subjects: LCSH: Rocky Mountain National Park (Colo.)--Juvenile literature. |
    National parks and reserves--Juvenile literature. | Rocky Mountains--Juvenile
    literature. | National parks and reserves--Colorado--Juvenile literature.

Classification: DDC 978.869--dc23

Table of Contents

Rocky Mountain National Park

Rocky Mountain National Park is in north-central Colorado. The park was signed into law by President Woodrow Wilson on January 26, 1915.

5

Nature & Natural Features

The park has four main zones. These zones are home to many different plants, animals, and natural features.

The **montane** zone is found between **elevations** of 5,600 and 9,500 feet (1,707 to 2,896 m). These are the lowest elevations in the park. For that reason, more plants and animals **thrive** in these areas.

Meadows filled with wildflowers are in the **montane** zone. Otters and beavers can be found in the rivers. Rocky mountain elk roam the open forests.

Between 9,000 and 11,000 feet (2,743 to 3,353 m) is the **subalpine** zone. Here, subalpine forests cover the mountainsides. The bark and needles of limber pine can handle this harsher environment.

Sprague Lake's beautiful, crystal clear water reflects its surroundings. Parry primrose grows in wet, rocky areas. Its bright pink flowers bloom after the snow melts.

15

The **alpine tundra** zone begins at 11,000 feet (3,353 m). The extreme weather makes survival difficult. Few plants and animals are tough enough to live here.

Perennials are the most common plant in the **alpine tundra**. The low-growing cushion plant escapes the strong winds.

19

Pikas are tiny **mammals** made for life in the **alpine tundra**. They feed on plants like alpine forget-me-not. They find shelter in piles of rock.

Fun Activities

Fish or fly-fish the more than 50 lakes and many streams in the park

Take a scenic drive through the many regions of the park

Walk some of the park's 355 miles (571 km) of hiking trails

Watch wildlife and try to spot a bighorn sheep

Glossary

alpine tundra – a natural area that contains no trees because it is at high elevation.

elevation – the height above sea level.

mammal – a warm-blooded animal with fur or hair on its skin and a skeleton inside its body.

montane – a natural area found in mountains. Dense forests are common at moderate elevations.

perennial – a plant that lives longer than two years.

subalpine – a natural area just below the tree line.

thrive – to do well and be strong and healthy.

Index